GREAT THOUGHTS FROM NAPOLEON

NAPOLEON

From the painting by Philippoteaux at Versailles

GREAT THOUGHTS FROM NAPOLEON

COMPILED BY
DR. A.S. RAPPOPORT

COSIMO CLASSICS

NEW YORK

Napoleon

The majority of the American reading public is acquainted with the history of Napoleon I. Everybody knows that he was the greatest military genius of modern times, and many are also aware of the fact that this Cæsar of modern Europe, this great conqueror, was also a great politician and first-rate administrator. But it will no doubt come as a surprise to a good many readers of this compilation to learn that Napoleon was also an author of considerable talent, a wonderful letter-writer, a philosopher, and a historian. Indeed, Nature seemed to have laid in the cradle of this wonder-child all her gifts, and to have showered upon Napoleon faculties and capabilities without number. He came into the world with a strong physique and a brain capable of a wonderful development; he had in him the stuff of the man of action and of thought—a combination rarely met, to such an extent at least, in other human beings. He had in him the love of art and of science, of action and of thought. He was one of those Titans of humanity who not only captivate the admiration of their contemporaries, but also command that of future generations. From a little corporal he rose to become artillery officer, general, First Consul of the French Republic, Emperor of the French and King of Italy, the mighty leader of legions, the Alexander of the West, carrying his victories from the banks of the Nile to those of the Moskva. But all through his feverish activity and his wonderful career the artist in Napoleon continued to dream, and his early ambition to write and wield the pen as he was wielding the sword never left him. His love of war and of battle was great; he was anxious to astonish Europe by some inimitable feats of arms; but his love of letters *was not less strong in him. He was one of the most charming and* spirituel *conversationalists, reminding one of Pascal, and always adapting himself to his audience, and his* milieu. *His time, however, was fully occupied in carrying out his gigantic plans, in creating an empire, and he could only express his thoughts in his own original style in his letters and despatches, in his proclamations and speeches. But they reveal, in addition to some of his earlier compositions, a considerable literary talent. But when this Prometheus had been chained upon his rock in the Atlantic, when the sword had been wrenched from his hand, then his great and secret ambition took hold with increased strength. He took up the pen and dictated his "Souvenirs" to Las Ceses, to Gourgaud, Montholon, and Bertrand. Like Cæsar and Sallust, the victor of Austerlitz became a luminous historian, coupled with a philosopher. His war maxims, his thoughts about men and things, his essays, revealed him to the world as a distinguished prose writer, as a man of letters, as an author of great merit, uniting in his style the brevity of Cæsar and the majestic solemnity of Livius. Napoleon's "Mémorial de Ste. Hélène" is a perfect mine of original sayings, terse and picturesque; and his "Œuvres littéraires" form several bulky volumes.*

A. S. RAPPOPORT.

Paris.

Like everything else in Corsica, my education was pitiful.

We have spoilt everything by treating women far too well. It was wrong of us to put them on a level with ourselves.

One pities those who have to play a part, especially when they can do without it.

I can meet fate and destiny with courage; and, unless I change, I shall very soon not move out of the way of a carriage.

At twenty-nine years of age I have exhausted everything. It now only remains for me to become a complete egoist.

It is very convenient to dictate one's thoughts. It is just as if one were holding a conversation.

Every one has his relative ideas. I have a predilection for founding, not for possessing.

You are very lucky; you need not make a spectacle of yourself. I am obliged to go about with a *cortège;* it is very boring, but it pleases the eye of the people.

I have never courted the applause of the Parisians. I am not an operatic monarch.

The lot of a dethroned king, who was born a king and nothing more, must be dreadful.

Death may expiate things, it does not repair them.

Manners are all in all to young females, and marriage is all they look for.

Greatness is nothing, if it is not lasting.

Financiers and bankers are often very useful. They manage to know everything.

The ideas of a Cabinet Minister should run quicker than his hand. He should put words in his letters and phrases in his words.

I do not believe that our nature is capable of entertaining a divided love; we are deceiving ourselves when we think we love two beings equally.

The true aristocracy must be ancient.

Chance is the providence of adventurers.

Men are like musicians at some concert; each has his own part to play.

The world needs nothing so much to promote her regeneration as good mothers.

Frenchmen do not know how to conspire.

The most tyrannical government is that which pretends to be paternal.

France and England, in alliance, might govern the world.

Imagination rules the world.

A woman requires six months in Paris to know what is her due and what is her sphere.

Sentiments are mostly traditionary.

Impossible! That word is not in the French dictionary.

There are calumnies against which innocence itself loses courage.

A State is lost when a woman is managing the public affairs.

I prefer more head and less tongue.

We cannot create men, and must use those we find.

The man born for office and authority sees nobody; he sees only things, their weight, and their consequence.

The greatest woman in the world is she who has borne the greatest number of children.

Mohammed's religion in ten years conquered half the known world, whilst it took three centuries for the religion of Christ to establish itself.

Christianity is too subtle for Orientals; they want something less spiritual, more definite.

The English are nothing but shop-keepers, and their glory consists in their wealth.

You must never mention insurrection to an Englishman; it frightens people in his country, where the people's party has been suppressed.

There is a greater number of honorable men, proportionately, in England than in any other country; and yet they have some very bad men there—they are in extremes.

Politics and sentiment never harmonize.

Women would do far better to work with their needles rather than with their tongues.

Old and corrupted nations cannot be governed on the same principles as those that are primitive, simple, and virtuous.

The true genius of the workman consists in making the right use of the materials at his disposal.

I frankly confess that if I must choose between oppression by the Bourbons and the violence of the mob, I much prefer the former.

Some philosopher has said that men are born wicked; it would be difficult and idle to discover whether his assertion is true.

The great mass of society is not wicked; if the majority were determined to be criminal, who could restrain or prevent them?

A beautiful woman pleases the eye, a good woman pleases the heart; the first is a jewel, the second a treasure.

It is in a Nation's workshops that war is most successfully waged against an enemy—and the engagement is bloodless.

When we have it in our power to speak emphatically and downrightly, why should we resort to cunning?

If my wife wants a thing done, it is a good reason for me to do the contrary.

Public opinion is always ready to prostitute itself to its own interests.

We must either strike or be stricken.

The surest way to gain the greatest influence over the decisions of princes is to wound their pride.

The allies we gain by success and victory turn against us upon the mere whisper of defeat.

Not every man is an atheist who would like to be.

A political club can have no permanent president; it requires one for each passion.

In war, as in love, ere we triumph we must come into contact.

A king is often obliged to commit crimes; they are the crimes of his position.

I multiplied myself by my activity.

The glory of the politician is to have his heart in his head.

To give way to despair without a struggle, and to end one's life as a relief, is like leaving the battlefield before the enemy is defeated.

Democracy elevates monarchy, aristocracy alone preserves it.

There is but one step from the sublime to the ridiculous.

Exiled kings never pardon on their return to the throne.

Empty stomachs know neither subordination nor fear.

Scepticism is a virtue in history as well as in philosophy.

Fortune is a woman—if you have missed her to-day, do not expect to meet her to-morrow.

Kings may not love as nurses do, tenderly.

To govern by a party is to put one's self sooner or later into its power.

I was never in love—except with Josephine, a little. Life is not worth giving to others.

The men who have changed the world never did so by gaining the rulers, but always by exciting the masses.

Marriage has not always been the consummation of love.

Kings and people are irreconcilable enemies.

In politics there is a long distance between promises and their fulfilment.

The police invent more than they detect.

There are no naked kings—there are only robed kings. Nature knows no kings; they are the result of civilization.

There are very few kings who have not deserved to be dethroned.

In marriage the beauty of the Venus de Medici should be only a secondary quality.

The only victory over love is flight.

The guilt of men is often only the result of their too great love for their wives.

The sympathy of a tottering nation can add no strength to an army.

It is the cause and not the death which makes the martyr.

Conscience is the inviolable asylum of the liberty of man.

Drama is the tragedy of women.

Divorce is a law in conformity with the interests of married people.

The only author who deserves to be read is he who never endeavors to influence and direct the opinion of the reader.

Nothing is done as long as anything still remains to be done.

England is said to traffic in everything. I should advise her to sell liberty, for which she could get a high price, and without any fear of exhausting her stock.

It is better that a people should have a bad organization than none at all.

We should laugh at men, so as to avoid crying for them.

Many a superior man is a child more than once a day.

Men are really not so ungrateful as people pretend; if one often hears complaints against them, it is because a benefactor usually expects more in return than he has given.

There are rattles for all ages.

Great men are like meteors; they shine and consume their light in order to enlighten the earth.

Kings can accomplish nothing; they are merely actors.

What is a throne? A bit of wood covered with velvet.

In all ages arts have been wedded to falsehood, and it is upon this basis that they flourish.

Cabinet Ministers may fall, but the nation remains.

A married man must be endowed with great firmness of character to be master of his family.

A priest should never throw off his cassock—he should never for a moment hide his real character.

When a man is determined to hold office under a government, he is already sold to the government.

The terrors of the next world have been imagined as a kind of supplement to the insufficient attractions which are presented to us in this.

Nations! Well do you deserve your chains and your ignominy!

Sometimes one battle decides everything, and sometimes a very insignificant circumstance decides a battle.

Paradise is a central spot where the souls of all men arrive by different routes. Each sect has its own particular path.

The Popes have committed too many
errors to be still considered infallible.

Psychology is not within the province
of generals of armies. They have only
to deal with the frame; what is beneath
the skin belongs to philosophers.

Poetry, painting, and sculpture must
lie; but they should lie with grandeur,
charm, and splendor.

Perfidy is generally individual, seldom
collective. Joseph's brothers could not
agree to take his life—Judas, coldly and
hypocritically, delivered his master unto
death.

A religion which relates to this life
alone, without telling man about his
origin and destination, is untenable.

Democracy may be furious, but it is not without pity and compassion.

A Minister of State should never allow a woman to approach his Cabinet.

Theology gives certain rules for spiritual government, but not for the government of armies and administration.

There are vices and virtues of circumstances.

A glutton will defend the morsel he has in his mouth like a hero.

What is government? Nothing, if it is not supported by opinion.

Virtue in woman has been suspected since the beginning of the world—and ever will be.

One must never count upon the people. They will cry indifferently: "Long live the king," and "Long live the conspirators."

One must have gone through as much as I have in order to be acquainted with all the difficulties of doing good.

We have done with the romance of the Revolution, let us now begin its history.

Ambassadors cost a lot of money but do very little.

Men are led by toys.

Remission of sins is a beautiful idea. It makes Christianity very attractive.

What a power would Christianity still have over humanity, did its ministers comprehend their mission!

A well-composed song softens the mind and produces a greater effect than a moral work which convinces our reason but does not warm our feelings.

The heart may sometimes be lacerated and yet the soul remain unshaken.

Do not talk to me of a religion which only takes me from this life without telling me whither I go.

When unable to arrange matters with God, one makes terms with the devil.

Clergymen consider this world only as a vehicle in which they can travel to another.

In war one sees one's own troubles— those of the enemy one cannot see.

If we were always to wait for the most favorable combination of circumstances no enterprise would ever be undertaken.

Fortune is a woman. The more she does for us the more we exact from her.

History should know how to catch men and nations as they would appear in the midst of their epoch.

It is not given to every man to appreciate honors only,—a little money is never
thrown away.

All the evils, all the scourges that can
afflict humanity, come from London.

Occupation is the scythe of time. A
man must fulfil his destinies. This is my
grand doctrine. Let mine be accom-
plished.

Why should I not view the future as I
view the past? Would the one power be
any more marvellous than the other?

A charlatan may say clever things, he
generally does—but he deludes us; his
conclusions are false.

Love is the occupation of the man of leisure, the distraction of the soldier, the stumbling-block of the monarch.

An empire such as France can very well afford to put up with a monastery or two of fools calling themselves "Trappists."

It is impossible to estimate the loss sustained by a State possessing ten thousand cloistered women.

Women should only be allowed to take the vow at fifty; at that age their task is done.

I do believe, not in religions, but in the idea of a God.

Convents attack the very roots of the population.

A dull and monotonous life inspires in the minds of certain men ideas which in a state of liberty had never entered their imagination.

Girls often marry in order to conform to the fashion.

There are more wives who abuse their husbands than husbands who abuse their wives.

So soon as a man is a king he is apart from all.

I know of nothing more terrible than a bad marriage or a dishonorable divorce.

In the married state one is surrounded by so many seductions.

Marriage is derived not from nature but from society and morality. An Eastern family is quite different from a Western family.

The English seem to prefer the bottle to the society of their women; after dinner they dismiss the ladies from the table and remain for hours drinking and intoxicating themselves.

Mutual dislike is not the cause of divorce, but the sign that divorce has become necessary.

Married people should be treated as minors, for their passions prevent them from letting their minds mature.

My desire is that girls may leave their school not agreeable women, but good women.

Anarchy always leads to absolute government.

Genius is no safeguard against the miseries of life.

Either I command or I hold my tongue.

You cannot make republics out of old monarchies.

I do not like your free thinkers: only fools defy mystery.

The special qualities of woman are beauty, charm, and seductiveness; her special obligations, dependence and submission.

Everything debases us except hatred.

Men are like units, they acquire their value chiefly by their position.

What would become of the bump of theft if there were no property?

Men, like pictures, require a favorable day.

Nothing better announces rank, education, and good breeding in a woman than the evenness of her disposition and her desire to please.

Out of a hundred favorites of kings, ninety-five are usually hanged.

Obedience has been imposed on the wife by the ancient laws: the angel imposed it on Eve.

A head without a memory is like a fort without a garrison.

Public morality is the natural complement of all laws; it is in itself a code.

He who takes the helm must support
the weight of it.

Every hour of time is a chance of mis-
fortune for future life.

The only useful faculty we have is ob-
servation.

I care nothing for the gossip of salons.
I know only one opinion of importance,
that of the rough peasant.

The populace is a tiger—when un-
muzzled.

It is with water and not with oil that one
quenches theological volcanoes.

Power is never ridiculous.

The religion of Jesus is a threat, that of Mohammed a promise.

The enthusiasm of others chills me.

The Austrians as a rule have no idea of the value of time.

The ceremony of baptism could never have originated in the West; water with us is not a sufficiently precious thing.

Spaciousness and immensity make us forget many a defect.

Cæsar, knowing the men who wanted to get rid of him, ought to have got rid of them first.

Pretty women need know no barriers, whatever they wish can happen.

My wife, you may dine with bankers— they are merchants dealing in money. But on no account would I have you go among shopkeepers, they are thieves stealing money.

Catherine II. was a master woman, worthy to grow a beard upon her chin.

Many a woman's toilet-table is a complete arsenal, for with supreme art she is defending herself against the assaults of time.

What might not be hoped from the English army, if each who behaved well had the chance of becoming a general some day?

The letters of Madame de Sévigné are like snow-eggs, one can eat plentifully of them without overloading the stomach.

I am nothing; I was a Mohammedan in Egypt, and I shall be a Catholic in France—for the welfare of the people.

If we are acquainted with our moral disease, we should treat our souls as we would our legs or our arms.

There is always a prejudice against those who hold the purse-strings.

Insanity is a degradation of human nature; I shall never go mad.

Bed has become for me a place of luxury. How fallen am I!

Create for us women who believe, not women logicians who can argue.

Aristocracy always remains cold. She never forgives.

In England the aristocracy are absolute masters, and the moment any reform threatens their power or privileges they raise the habitual cry: "The foundations of the constitution are being destroyed."

You may call me what you please; you
cannot prevent me from being myself.

A fall usually has the effect of lowering
a man's character. But, on the contrary,
my fall has elevated me prodigiously.

Christianity is a spiritual, Islam a sen-
sual religion. The former is a religion
of menaces and fears, the latter of promises and attractions.

Constitutions are the work of time, we
must leave ample room for ameliorations.

Fanaticism should be lulled to sleep before it is eradicated.

A man, to be really great, no matter in what order of greatness, must have improvised a portion of his own glory, and shown himself superior to the event which he has brought about.

Force remains always force, enthusiasm is nothing but enthusiasm, but persuasion remains engraved in the hearts.

Religion is a sort of vaccination; while satisfying our love of the marvellous, it guarantees us against charlatans and sorcerers.

After all, priests are worth more than all the Cagliostros, all the Kants, and all the dreamers of Germany.

Shakespeare had been forgotten in England for two centuries; Voltaire, who lived in Geneva, and who wished to flatter Englishmen of his acquaintance, praised him, and everybody began to repeat that Shakespeare was the greatest poet in the world.

Everything in life is a matter of calculation, one must know how to hold the balance between good and evil.

A congress is a fable agreed upon by politicians. It is the pen of Machiavelli united to the sword of Mohammed.

Political equilibrium is only a dream.

Nothing is so imperious as weakness which knows itself supported by strength.

The best means of obtaining credit is never to ask for it.

Woman has no thought but for pleasure and for dress.

There are no absolutely fearless people among those who have something to lose.

Many people are virtuous simply because they lack the opportunity for vice.

People as a rule make use of their memory much more frequently than of their judgment.

Deliberative assemblies are always composed of intriguers.

When bayonets deliberate, the power escapes from the hands of the government.

If political mistakes were a crime in the eyes of God, no sovereign would meet with pardon.

The mere mention of rights of the people under a despotic government is blasphemy and a crime.

There is no absolute despotism, it is always relative.

We must know how to give before we take.

Enemies likely to be dangerous are clever enough never to expose themselves to danger.

A great people may be killed, but not intimidated.

One may undertake everything with audacity, but not do everything.

In war there is only one favorable moment; the great talent of the commander consists in seizing it.

War is like government, it is a question of tact.

Ambition is to man what air is to nature —take away the one or the other and there will be no movement.

An enemy is much more anxious to do you harm than a friend is to be useful.

With my sword by my side, and the works of Homer in my pocket, I hope to push my way through the world.

Despotism, passing from the hands of the rulers into those of the subjects, always remains despotism.

Republican despotism abounds in acts of tyranny, because every citizen has his hand in it.

We should endeavor to discover the human weaknesses, and try to adapt ourselves to them rather than oppose them.

Marriage ought not to be allowed between individuals who have known one another for only six months.

Other people's follies never serve to make us wise.

Frenchmen love greatness and admire even the semblance of it.

In order to do something great, one must have either faithful friends or bitter enemies.

There is nothing worse than honest people in a political crisis, especially when their conscience is fascinated by false ideas.

Humanity is grateful to those who astonish her.

The ambitious are like lovers, possession diminishes their ardor.

Many things are called legitimate simply because they are old.

In politics, justice is nothing but force in the garb of virtue.

Political liberty is, after all, nothing but a fable, invented by those who rule, to lull to sleep those who are being ruled.

What we call natural law is nothing but the law of interest and reason.

It would be a curious book in which there were no lies.

For one woman who inspires us to do something good, there are a hundred who lead us into folly.

Poor nations! In spite of your wisdom and your experience, you are swayed by the caprices of fashion like simple individuals.

'Among those who protest against being oppressed there are many who are fond of oppressing.

When nations cease to complain, it is a sign that they have ceased to think.

Absolute government has no need to tell lies—it is silent. Representative government, obliged to speak, disguises the truth, and lies with impunity.

A fool has always one advantage over a clever man—he is always self-satisfied.

Theology is to religion what poisons are to food.

Vice is as necessary to society as storms are to the atmosphere. If the balance between good and evil is disturbed, the harmony is broken and revolution is the result.

The vulgar judge the influence of a courtier by the number of his valets; the populace judges the power of God by the number of His priests.

Had one of our contemporaries written the *Iliad*, nobody would appreciate it.

The times of *rois fainéants* (lazy kings) are past.

Revolutions are like dirty dunghills—they bring into growth the noblest vegetables.

Independence, like honor, is a rocky island without a beach.

In politics a man must have a conventional conscience.

There are men who have strength enough of mind to change their characters, or at least to yield to imperative circumstances.

In religion everything should be gratu-
itous. One should not deprive the poor,
because they are poor, of the only thing
which consoles them for their poverty.

Religion is of great importance in a
girls' public school; it is the safest guar-
antee for mothers and husbands.

Women would lay claim to an equality
with men. It is pure folly. Woman is
man's property; man is not woman's. A
woman gives a man children; a man does
not give a woman children.

Man, and above all the historian, is full
of vanity. He gives fine scope to his imagination, and tries to interest the reader
at the expense of truth.

Theology, as long as it only limits itself to speculative facts, is good and even useful; but as soon as, repudiating its tendencies, it dives into politics and government, it is liable to commit many follies.

It is difficult to escape the arbitrariness of the judge, unless by placing one's self under the despotism of the law.

Laws, beautifully clear in theory, often become a perfect chaos in practice.

Everything has a limit, even human passions.

There is no constitution in the world which is followed to the letter.

During a political storm the constitution of the people serves them as a polar star.

Doctors and priests should always remain so; they ought to be free from all political bias.

It is better to run the risk of having one master than to have a thousand.

I am not a person, I am a thing.

When you have to make your choice, it is better to devour than to be devoured.

I have fought like a lion for the Republic, and by way of recompense it grants me permission to die of hunger.

A couple of hours passed on the boards places the actor in the presence of a public which dispenses glory.

Nobody has conceived anything great in our century; it falls to my lot to give the example.

It is not genius which suddenly and secretly reveals unto me what I have to say or do—it is my own meditation and reflection.

The rabble deserve nothing but contempt; only as a last resource should one attack them.

I am always the same; men of my stamp never change.

Remember that the world was created
in only six days. Ask of me whatever
you like, except time—it is the only thing
beyond my power.

Is not theology reserved for Heaven?
Why make God here below the subject of
our discussions?

Great men are never cruel without
necessity.

Blood-letting is one of the remedies in
political medicine.

Do you imagine that it was Luther who
brought about the Reformation? No; it
was public opinion which was in opposition
to the Popes.

Love should be a pleasure, not a torment.

Egoism is of later birth than love. At forty a man loves his fortune, at eighty himself.

I have always admired Mithridates contemplating the conquest of Rome when he was vanquished and a fugitive.

Love is a man's statement at once of his impotence and of his immortality.

The finest eyes in the world—and there are some very fine eyes here—will not make me deviate a hair's breadth from the plan I have traced.

He who is master of Egypt is master of India.

Hortense (Queen of Holland) forces me to believe in feminine virtue.

It will scarcely be believed that when, upon one occasion, I met Madame du Colombier, my first love, all our happiness consisted in our eating cherries together.

I have failed, and therefore I was in the wrong—it is only justice.

There are people who really believe in their talent to govern simply because they are governing.

It is not by playing and dancing that a man is to be moulded.

There are vices and virtues which depend upon circumstances.

In my council there were men possessed of much more eloquence than I was; I always defeated them by this simple argument: two and two make four.

Kings nowadays require more security than peoples.

Mohammed appeared at a moment when all men were anxious to be authorized to believe in only one God.

Madame de Staël teaches thinking to people who have either never thought before or have forgotten how to think.

The English are in everything more practical than the French; they emigrate, marry, kill themselves, with less indecision than the French display in going to the opera.

Vanity lay at the bottom of the French Revolution.

Russia, if you are not careful, will be laying down the law for all of you.

I do not believe in the proverb that in order to be able to command one must know how to obey.

My policy is to govern the people as the greatest number wish to be governed.

To attempt to regenerate a people in a day would be an act of madness.

Nothing is more damaging to morality than the law which makes divorce impossible.

There was the instinct of true policy in Alexander's ideas of making himself out to be the descendant of a god.

Good nature is an affectation which a sovereign ought to avoid.

I wish I had conversed a great deal more with women. They would have told me many things which men would not relate to me.

As long as people do not learn from their infancy whether they ought to be republicans or monarchists, the State will never form a nation.

The only true conquests, and those which awaken no regret, are the conquests obtained over ignorance.

The first element of the well-being of a nation consists in the just equilibrium between the amount of taxes imposed for the maintenance of public revenue and the surplus of the price of its labor.

Ancient Greece boasted of seven wise men; I find none in Europe.

You are young, and know not what political hatred is.

In politics nothing is good or bad in itself, but according to the party to which one belongs.

England, which the economists who preach freedom of trade constantly quote as a model, is in reality the country of prohibitions.

When a man goes to sleep in his position, it is time he were superseded.

The work of destruction is the work of an instant, but it requires the help of time to rebuild.

The country possesses many clever men; what is required is to find them and to put them in their proper stations. One is at the plough who ought to be in the council, and another is minister who ought to be at the plow.

Equality delights the multitude, while liberty is needed only by a small and privileged class, and can therefore be restricted with impunity.

What I did is immense. What I had decided to do, and what I had projected, were still more so.

A world might be created with budgets.

A sovereign's first duty is, no doubt, to conform to the wishes of his people. But what the people say is hardly ever what they wish.

When a king is said to be good, his reign is a failure.

The French are what the Gauls were: fierce and fickle. They have one fetich: honor. They must have distinctions. See how they bow before the stars of strangers!

Music is the tender companion of emotional man, the inspirer of sentiment.

Religion is the dominion of the soul, the hope of life, the anchor of safety, and the deliverance from evil.

The drum is the best of all musical instruments; it never goes out of tune.

Fighting is a soldier's religion—I never changed that. The other is the affair of women and priests. As for myself, I always adopt the religion of the country I am in.

If I governed a community of Jews, I would rebuild the temple of Solomon.

When one man is dying of hunger near
another who is suffering from superabun-
dance of wealth, he can scarcely resign
himself to this difference, unless there is
an authority that can say to him, "God
wills it so."

Religion is not freemasonry.

To say whence we come, what we are,
whither we go, is beyond our thoughts,
and yet the thing exists. We are the
watches which exist, but do not know.

With me immortality is the recollection
one leaves in the memory of man.

It was not the Roman army which conquered Gaul, but Cæsar; it was not the Carthaginian army which, before the gates of Rome, made the Eternal City tremble, but Hannibal.

I have never usurped a crown; I found it in the gutter and put it upon my head.

After all, should a great statesman have any feeling? Is he not a completely eccentric personage, standing always alone on his own side, with the world on the other?

Nothing is attained in war except by calculation.

A physician ought to look upon himself as belonging to no nation in particular.

Obedience to rules does not insure success, but success furnishes a canon of conduct.

Tragedy should be the school of kings and peoples.

Misfortunes are not without their heroism and their glory. Adversity was the one thing wanting in my career.

Printing seems to act as the seal of authority. Written documents do not produce upon the public the same effect as those that are printed.

Madness is the last stage of human degradation.

An oligarchy yields to nothing but force.

Ceremonies are to religion what external garments are to men in power.

The common men seek out the great, not for themselves, but for their influence; and the latter welcome them out of vanity.

The most insupportable of tyrannies is that of inferiors.

I am not an ordinary man, and the laws of morality and custom have therefore never been made for me.

The remarks of a fool teach us to what degree of simplicity we must descend so as to be understood by all.

Sovereigns only love people who are useful to them—and only so long as they are useful.

It is easier to establish a republic without anarchy than a monarchy without despotism.

It is not easy to obtain simplicity from lawyers.

Fools are only troublesome, pedants unbearable.

The world is a comedy where one finds 100,000 Tartuffes for one Molière.

Indecision in a ruler is to government what paralysis is to the motion of the members.

Chance is the only lawful monarch of the universe.

Nineteen-twentieths of those in power do not believe in morality; but they consider it their interest that people should be convinced that they are making good use of their power. Thereby alone they are called honorable.

In politics partners are required, otherwise the play cannot be enacted.

Babbling is a national characteristic of the French since the days of the Gauls.

I have never been led astray by prosperity. Adversity would find me out of her reach.

I love you more and more every day. This shows that La Bruyère was wrong when he said, "Love comes of a sudden." Love, like everything in nature, has to run its course, and has a definite rate of growth.

I can no longer recognize my obscure relations. Those who will not rise with me, I shall no longer be able to consider of my family.

Man is always ready to leave that which lies in front of him for that which is manufactured in the skies.

A man occupied with public business cannot attend to orthography. His ideas must flow faster than his hand can trace. He has only time to place his points.

COSIMO is an innovative publisher of books that inspire, inform, and engage readers worldwide.

COSIMO was inspired by Cosimo de Medici, the first of the de Medici dynasty, who ignited the most important cultural and artistic revolution in Western history — the Renaissance.

Cosimo de Medici, the quintessential Renaissance man, was a banker, political leader, scholar, and patron of the arts. He had a passion for the pursuit of knowledge, and he breathed new life into the study of the ancient past. He enriched Florence by building palaces and churches and by sponsoring libraries, where professional scribes copied classics from antiquity into the finest manuscripts.

This quest for enrichment is the foundation for **COSIMO,** an innovative publisher of books that inspire, inform, and engage readers worldwide. **COSIMO CLASSICS** brings to life unique, out-of-print classics, representing subjects as diverse as *Alternative Health, Business and Economics, Eastern Philosophy, Personal Growth, Mythology, Philosophy, Sacred Texts, Science, Spirituality,* and much more!

COSIMO CLASSICS uses state-of-the art technology to publish distinctive, high-quality books that are always available online at affordable prices.

COSIMO CLASSICS uses state-of-the-art technology to publish distinctive, high-quality books. In our pursuit for enrichment, our commitment to you is that **COSIMO CLASSICS** offers:

> **Permanent Availability:** Our books never go out of print.

> **Global Availability**: Our books are available online at www.cosimobooks.com, www.amazon.com, www.barnesandnoble.com, and other online bookstores, and can be ordered from your favorite local bookstore, too.

> **Special Quantity Discounts:** Our books are available at special quantity discounts for bulk purchases, sales promotions, premiums, or fund raising. For more information, please contact us at info@cosimobooks.com.

> **Free e-Newsletter:** Sign up for our e-newsletter at www.cosimobooks.com to discover what's happening at **COSIMO** and to receive announcements of our new books, free excerpts, and special offers.

Your Favorite Out-of-Print Books: If you know of any books that you would like to see republished as a **COSIMO CLASSIC**, drop us a line at info@cosimobooks.com.

A complete collection of **COSIMO CLASSICS** is always available at our website, www.cosimobooks.com.